MOMMY, I WANT TO BE A VET!

ESPERANZA RIVERA

To order additional copies of this book, contact:
Xlibris
1-888-795-4274
www.Xlibris.com
Orders@Xlibris.com

TO ALL PARENTS WHO HELP NURTURE
THEIR CHILDREN'S DREAMS.

TO ALL MY FAMILY AND FRIENDS WHO SUPPORTED CHRISTEE IN PURSUIT OF HER DREAM, THOSE WHO GAVE HER WORDS OF ENCOURAGEMENT, THOSE WHO DROVE HER TO FEED HER ANIMALS BEFORE SHE COULD DRIVE ON WEEKENDS AND HOLIDAYS. THOSE WHO HELPED HER CLEAN THE STABLES, THOSE WHO WENT TO COMPETITION, AND THOSE WHO CHEERED HER ON ALL HER LIFE.

"WHAT A NOBLE AND COURAGEOUS CAREER, DEAR! WILL IT BE THE ARMY, THE MARINE CORPS, THE NAVY, THE AIR FORCE? OR IS IT THE COAST GUARD, MY DEAR?"

"*HUH!*" "*WHAT?*" CHRISTEE REPLIED AND SOUNDED VERY CONFUSED. "NO, MOMMY. I WANT TO BE A VETERAN!" "YES, DEAR, BUT BEFORE YOU CAN BE A VETERAN, YOU MUST JOIN ONE OF THE ARMED SERVICES," MOMMY EXPLAINED. BUT CHRISTEE BLURTED OUT, "TO BE A DOCTOR FOR PUPPIES, YOU HAVE TO BE A SOLDIER FIRST?"

WITH A PUZZLED FACE AND HER HANDS ON HER HIPS,
CHRISTEE SAID, "I JUST WANT TO BE A DOCTOR."
"A DOCTOR FOR LITTLE PUPPIES, CUTE LITTE PUPPIES

AND DANCING ONES TOO,

OR BEAR LOOKING ONES,

PLAYFUL AND LAZY,

OR WRESTLING ONES TOO!

A VETERAN, MOM! NOW DO YOU UNDERSTAND ME?"
AND CHRISTEE CONTINUED "A DOCTOR FOR **BIG**

AND LITTLE ANIMALS!"

MOMMY LAUGHED, HUGGED HER, AND SAID, "DEAR, YOU MEAN, YOU WANT TO BE A VET·ER·I·NAR·I·AN?"

VET ER I NAR I AN [VET·ER·I·NAR·I·AN |VE-TƏ-RƏ-ˈNER-Ē-ƏN] A PERSON WHO IS TRAINED TO GIVE MEDICAL CARE AND TREATMENT TO ANIMALS.

CHRISTEE SHRUGGED AND SAID, "*HUH? WHAT DO YOU MEAN?*" "A DOCTOR FOR LITTLE PUPPIES, KITTENS, BUNNIES, AND ALL CREATURES IS CALLED A **VETERINARIAN?**"

"YES," MOMMY REPLIED.

CHRISTEE GIGGLED AND SAID, "THAT IS WHAT I WANT, AND I WILL BE SOMEDAY!"

(CHRISTEE WAS ONLY IN THE SECOND GRADE AND ALREADY KNEW WHAT SHE WANTED TO BE WHEN SHE GREW UP.)

"WHAT A NOBLE CAREER!" MOMMY REPLIED.

AS CHRISTEE GREW UP, HER LOVE FOR ANIMALS GREW TOO. SHE TOOK IN *ALL KINDS OF* STRAYS:

CATS

BABY CHICKS

BUNNIES

AND EVEN A BABY POSSUM,

WHICH, OF COURSE, SHE BATHED AND CLEANED BECAUSE IT WAS FULL OF FLEAS!

MOMMY WOULD SAY, MAKING A DISAPPROVING FACE AND WAGGING HER FINGER IN A DISAPPROVING MANNER, "CHRISTEE, THIS IS NOT A ZOO. FIND THEM A HOME." CHRITEE WOULD ALWAYS FIND A GOOD HOME FOR THEM.

SHE CONTINUED TO GROW WITH A COMMITMENT TO HER ANIMALS AND HER DREAM TO BE A VETERINARIAN.

AND THEN SHE ANNOUNCED, "MOM, I AM GOING TO A HIGH SCHOOL THAT HAS AN AGRICULTURE PROGRAM, WHICH WILL ALLOW ME TO RAISE A FARM ANIMAL EVERY YEAR AND EVEN COMPETE IN THE ANNUAL COUNTY FAIR."

CHRISTEE FEEDING HER LAMB AND EXPLAINING TO DUSTEE, HER DOG, HOW SPECIAL THEY BOTH WERE TO HER.

CHRISTEE TRAINING HER LAMB

CHRISTEE COMPETING

LIKE MANY YEARS BEFORE, WHEN DUSTEE BROKE A LEG, SHE TOOK HER TO THE VETERINARIAN, AND THEY TRAINED HER ON HOW TO TAKE CARE OF HER. OR WHEN HER COUSIN'S DOG WAS NOT BREATHING, SHE GAVE IT CPR, AND YEAH, SHE EVEN PUT A SPLINT ON A MOUSE THAT HER DOG HAD CAUGHT.

NOTHING THAT THOSE LITTLE ANIMALS EVER DID WAS UNPLEASANT OR UNLOVING.

THE LITTLE GIRL HAD BECOME A YOUNG WOMAN, AND HER LOVE FOR ANIMALS GREW AND GREW, AND HER DREAM OF BEING A VETERINARIAN NEVER WAVERED.

NOW MOMMY IMAGINES HER LITTLE GIRL TAKING CARE OF
GOD'S LITTLE ANIMALS AND ALL HIS CREATURES IN HEAVEN.

THE END.

EPILOGUE

What happened to Christee's dream?

Life happened. The illness that she had developed while in high school took her life, but not her spirit, not her courage, and not her dream. Her dream was present even in the last few weeks of her life.

While at UCLA Hospital, she refused to accept and submit a doctor's excuse and insisted to take her final college exams.

"Mom, I have to take the finals. I am about to graduate and then vet school. I do not want to delay not one more day," she explained.

And she took her final exams there at the hospital. The doctors and nurses were amazed at her courage and dedication in reaching her dream. However, God had a different plan!

I did not want to put the sad ending of Christee's dream in the story. It is up to you, the parent, to decide whether you want to tell your children about Christee's perseverance and courage despite her illness. It is up to you to teach them about grieving and healing. As for me, Christee has fulfilled her dream in heaven.

THIS IS BASED ON A TRUE STORY, TO LEARN ABOUT
CHRISTEE'S FULL STORY, READ *"A WITNESS OF MIRACLES"* BY
ESPERANZA RIVERA OR VISIT ESPERANZARIVERA.COM.

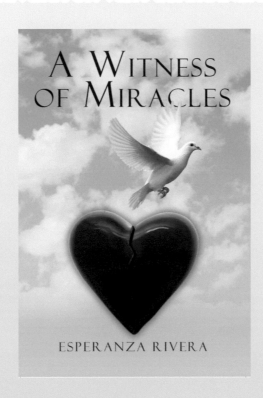

Printed in the United States
By Bookmasters